THE ROYAL
HORTICULTURAL
SOCIETY

A GARDENER'S
FIVE YEAR
RECORD BOOK

F
FRANCES LINCOLN LIMITED
PUBLISHERS

Frances Lincoln Limited
4 Torriano Mews
Torriano Avenue
London NW5 2RZ
www.franceslincoln.com

The Royal Horticultural Society A Gardener's Five Year Record Book
Copyright © Frances Lincoln Limited 2006 and 2008

Text and illustrations copyright © the Royal Horticultural Society 2006
and 2008
Printed under licence granted by the Royal Horticultural Society,
Registered Charity no. 2228789/SCO38262
For more information visit our website or call 0845 130 4646.

An interest in gardening is all you need to enjoy being a member
of the RHS.

Website: www.rhs.org.uk

A catalogue record for this book is available from the British Library

ISBN: 978-0-7112-2856-6

Printed in China
First Frances Lincoln edition 2006
This revised edition 2008

9 8 7 6 5 4 3 2

Front cover
Papaver rhoeas (left) and Papaver somniferum (right)

Back cover
Primula auricula

Title page
Tulip cultivars

Right
The giant sunflower (Helianthus giganteus)

INTRODUCTION

The illustrations in this book have been taken from the *Phytanthoza Iconographia* (1737–45), the first botanical work published on the continent of Europe to be printed in colour.

The work was compiled by Johann Wilhelm Weinmann (1683–1741), a wealthy apothecary in Regensburg, Germany, who built up a fine collection of botanical art. In the 1730s Weinmann put his collection to use by financing a major publication based on it. The work is in four volumes, alphabetically arranged, and because it was based on a collection of drawings, it is diverse in its styles of illustration. The plates were engraved by Bartholomaeus Seuter and Johann Elias Ridinger, with additions by Johann Jakob Haid. None of the original artists is named but some of the plates may be based on unsigned drawings by Georg Dionysius Ehret (1708–70), one of the greatest botanical artists, whose first important patron was Weinmann. The subtle colours achieved in the mezzotint engravings make the *Phytanthoza* possibly the finest of early colour-printed books.

We hope that you will enjoy making this beautiful book into a growing treasury of notes, observations, plans and reflections, and that it will be a valuable gardening assistant and companion over the next five years and beyond.

Brent Elliott
The Royal Horticultural Society

JANUARY

	YEAR	
WEATHER	19/1 Hard frost	
PLANTS IN BLOOM		
TASKS		
NOTES	Hall windowsill 19/1 seen 10 germinated 11 4D x 1	

Hyacinth cultivar (*Hyacinthus orientalis*)

JANUARY

JANUARY

	YEAR		
WEATHER			
PLANTS IN BLOOM			
TASKS			
NOTES			

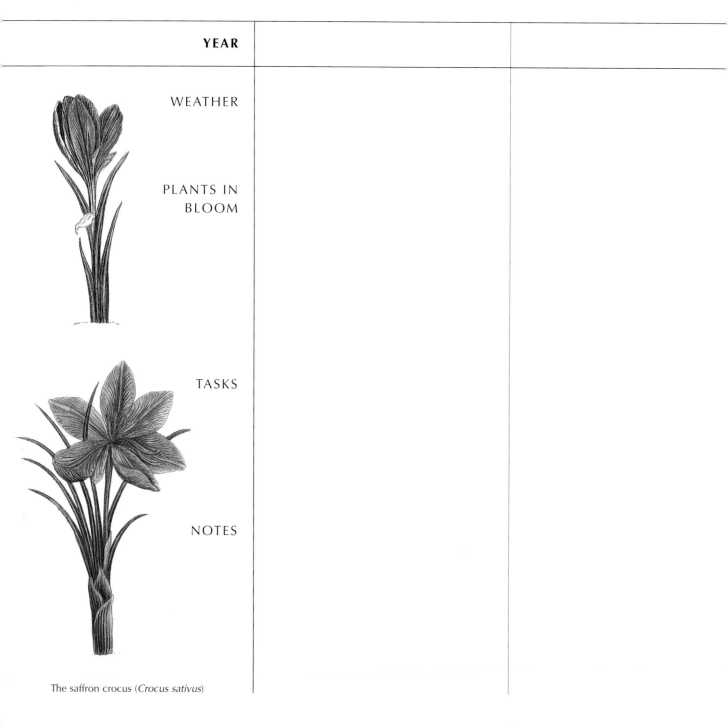

The saffron crocus (*Crocus sativus*)

JANUARY

JANUARY

	YEAR		
WEATHER			
PLANTS IN BLOOM			
TASKS			
NOTES			

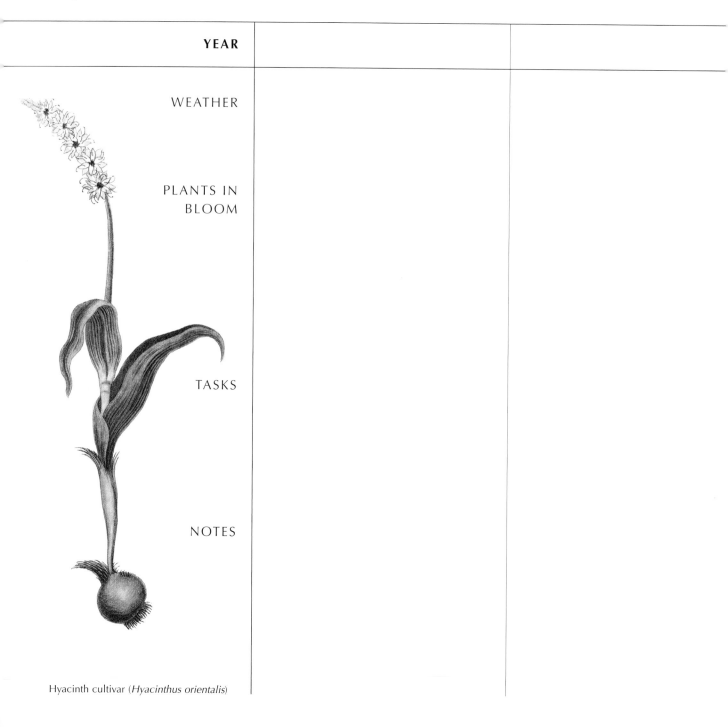

Hyacinth cultivar (*Hyacinthus orientalis*)

JANUARY

JANUARY

YEAR		
WEATHER		
PLANTS IN BLOOM		
TASKS		
NOTES		

Auricula cultivars (*Primula* x *auricula*)

JANUARY

JANUARY

	YEAR		
WEATHER			
PLANTS IN BLOOM			
TASKS			
NOTES			

Muscari botryoides forms

JANUARY

FEBRUARY

	YEAR		
WEATHER			
PLANTS IN BLOOM			
TASKS			
NOTES			

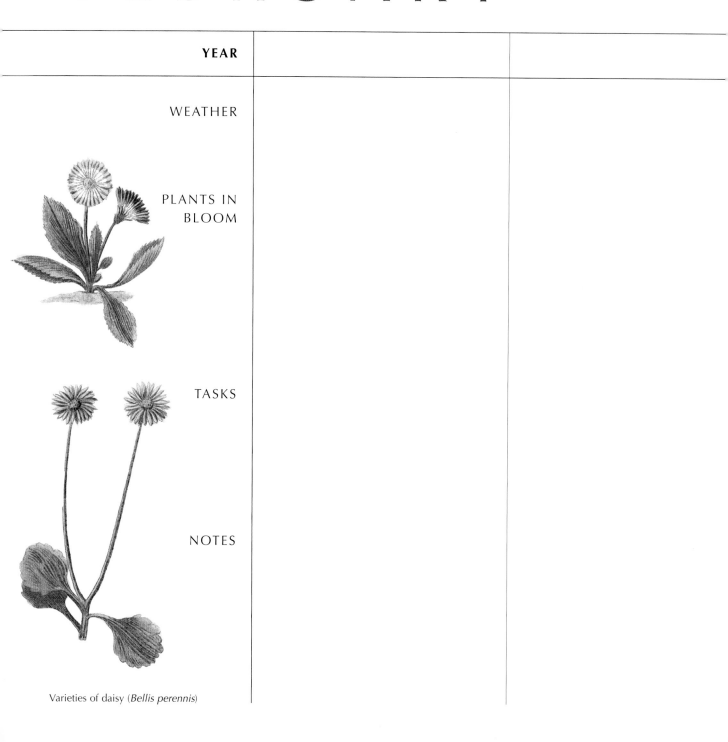

Varieties of daisy (*Bellis perennis*)

FEBRUARY

FEBRUARY

	YEAR		
WEATHER			
PLANTS IN BLOOM			
TASKS			
NOTES			

The saffron crocus (*Crocus sativus*)

FEBRUARY

FEBRUARY

YEAR		
WEATHER		
PLANTS IN BLOOM		
TASKS		
NOTES		

Varieties of daisy (*Bellis perennis*)

FEBRUARY

FEBRUARY

	YEAR		
WEATHER			
PLANTS IN BLOOM			
TASKS			
NOTES			

Cultivars of primrose

FEBRUARY

FEBRUARY

	YEAR		
WEATHER			
PLANTS IN BLOOM			
TASKS			
NOTES			

Adonis annua

FEBRUARY

MARCH

WEATHER

PLANTS IN
BLOOM

TASKS

NOTES

Rush-leaved jonquil (*Narcissus assoanus*)

MARCH

MARCH

	YEAR		
WEATHER			
PLANTS IN BLOOM			
TASKS			
NOTES			

Jonquils (*Narcissus jonquilla*)

MARCH

MARCH

	YEAR		
WEATHER			
PLANTS IN BLOOM			
TASKS			
NOTES			

Anemone cultivars

MARCH

MARCH

	YEAR		
WEATHER			
PLANTS IN BLOOM			
TASKS			
NOTES			

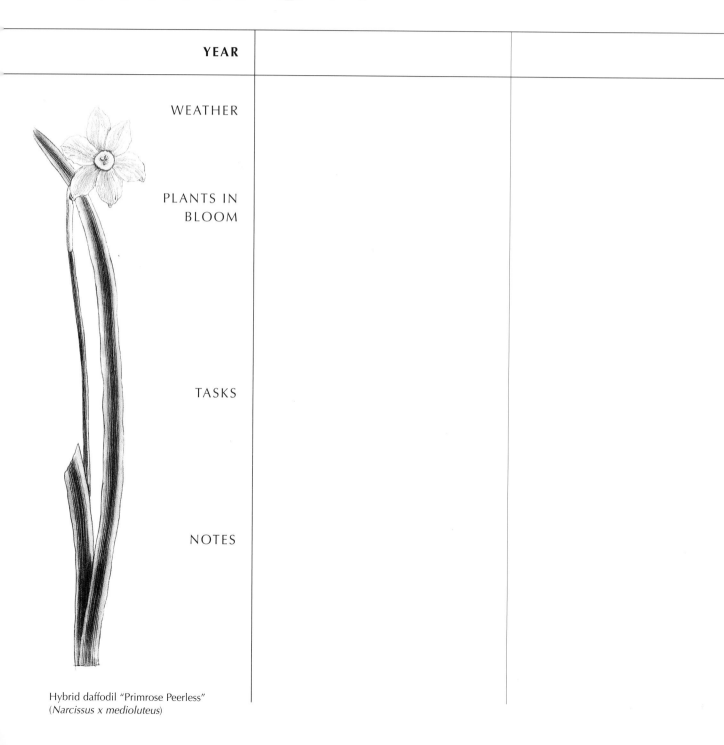

Hybrid daffodil "Primrose Peerless"
(*Narcissus x medioluteus*)

MARCH

MARCH

YEAR		
WEATHER		
PLANTS IN BLOOM		
TASKS		
NOTES		

Fritillaria meleagris forms

MARCH

APRIL

	YEAR		
WEATHER			
PLANTS IN BLOOM			
TASKS			
NOTES			

Onion cultivar (*Allium cepa*)

APRIL

APRIL

	YEAR		
WEATHER			
PLANTS IN BLOOM			
TASKS			
NOTES			

Onion cultivar (*Allium cepa*)

APRIL

APRIL

	YEAR		
WEATHER			
PLANTS IN BLOOM			
TASKS			
NOTES			

Tulip cultivar

APRIL

APRIL

	YEAR		
WEATHER			
PLANTS IN BLOOM			
TASKS			
NOTES			

Iris cultivar

APRIL

APRIL

YEAR		
WEATHER		
PLANTS IN BLOOM		
TASKS		
NOTES		

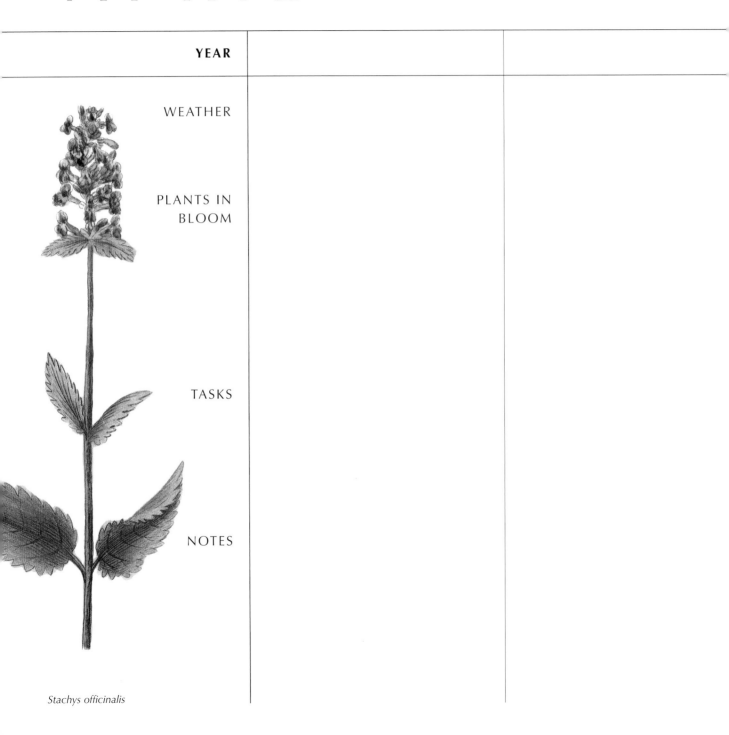

Stachys officinalis

APRIL

MAY

YEAR		
WEATHER		
PLANTS IN BLOOM		
TASKS		
NOTES		

Tulip cultivar

MAY

MAY

YEAR

WEATHER

PLANTS IN
BLOOM

TASKS

NOTES

Iris cultivars

MAY

MAY

	YEAR		
WEATHER			
PLANTS IN BLOOM			
TASKS			
NOTES			

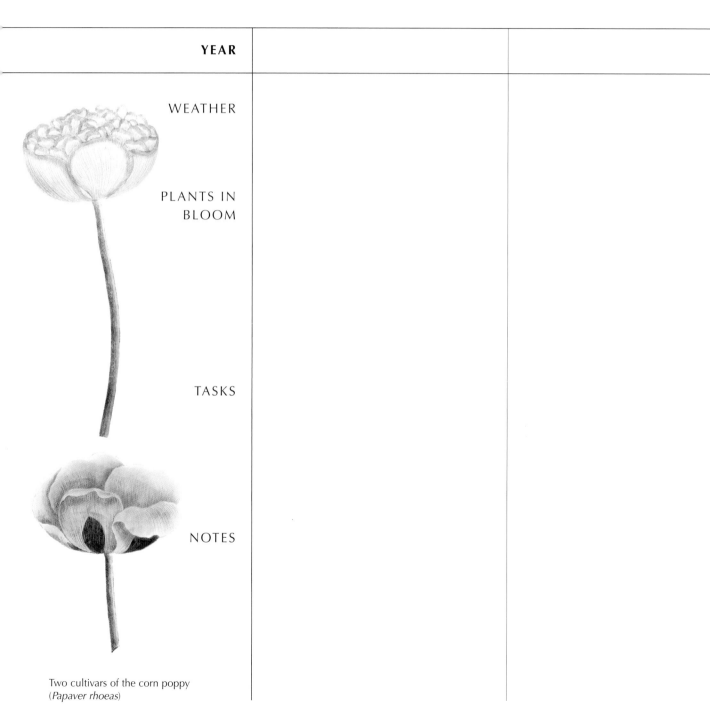

Two cultivars of the corn poppy
(*Papaver rhoeas*)

MAY

MAY

	YEAR		
WEATHER			
PLANTS IN BLOOM			
TASKS			
NOTES			

Two rose cultivars from the eighteenth century, then called 'Milesia' and 'Passe d'Angleterre'

MAY

MAY

	YEAR		
WEATHER			
PLANTS IN BLOOM			
TASKS			
NOTES			

Aquilegia vulgaris var *stellata*

MAY

JUNE

YEAR		
WEATHER		
PLANTS IN BLOOM		
TASKS		
NOTES		

Flowers of tobacco (*Nicotiana*)

JUNE

JUNE

	YEAR		
WEATHER			
PLANTS IN BLOOM			
TASKS			
NOTES			

Clove pinks (*Dianthus caryophyllus*)

JUNE

J U N E

	YEAR		
WEATHER			
PLANTS IN BLOOM			
TASKS			
NOTES			

The rusty foxglove (*Digitalis ferruginea*)

JUNE

JUNE

YEAR		
WEATHER		
PLANTS IN BLOOM		
TASKS		
NOTES		

A rose cultivar from the eighteenth century

JUNE

JUNE

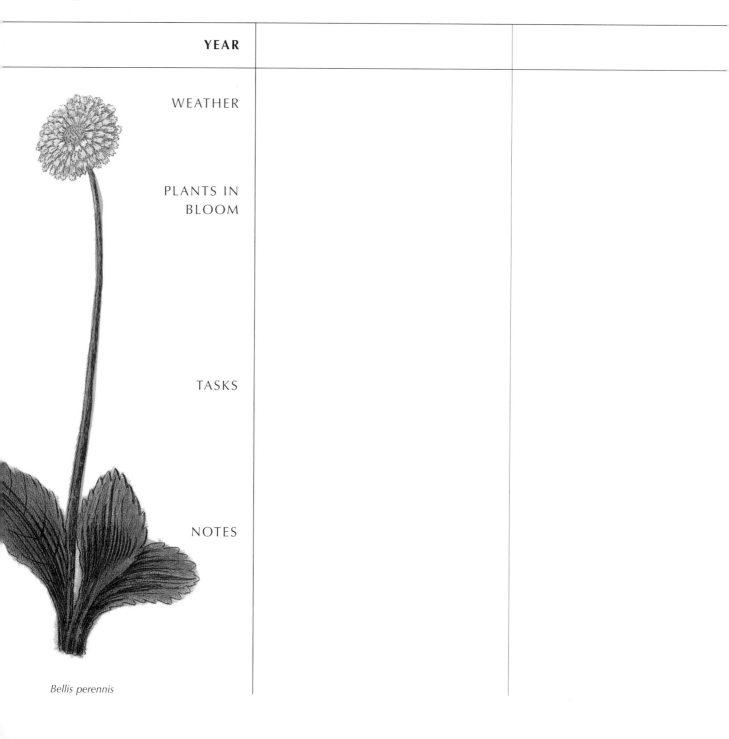

YEAR		
WEATHER		
PLANTS IN BLOOM		
TASKS		
NOTES		

Bellis perennis

JUNE

JULY

YEAR		
WEATHER		
PLANTS IN BLOOM		
TASKS		
NOTES		

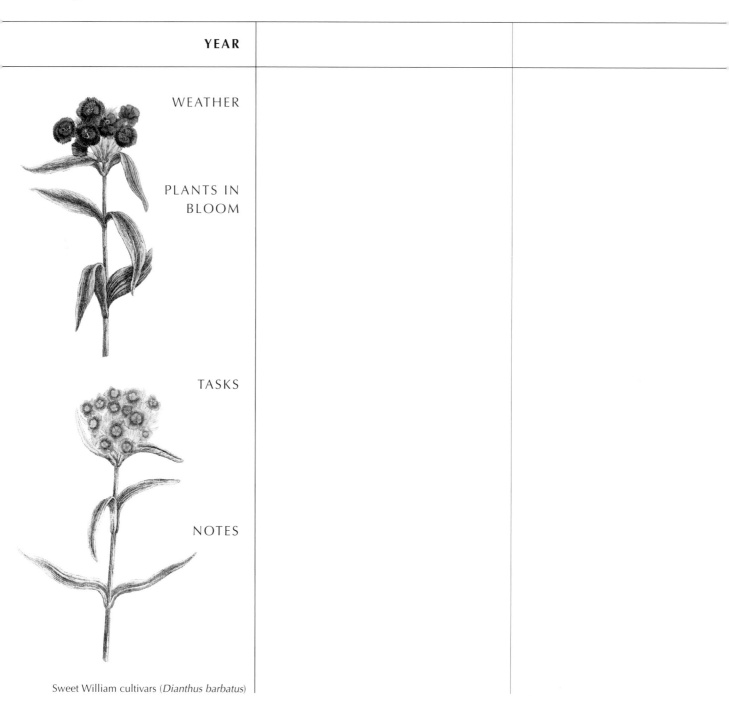

Sweet William cultivars (*Dianthus barbatus*)

JULY

JULY

	YEAR		
WEATHER			
PLANTS IN BLOOM			
TASKS			
NOTES			

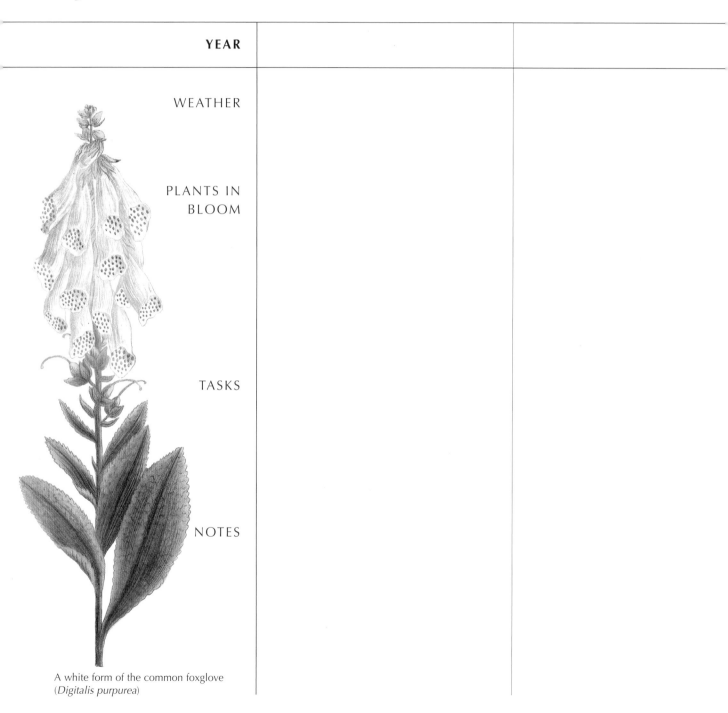

A white form of the common foxglove
(*Digitalis purpurea*)

JULY

YEAR		
WEATHER		
PLANTS IN BLOOM		
TASKS		
NOTES		

Cornflower cultivars (*Centaurea montana*)

JULY

JULY

YEAR		
WEATHER		
PLANTS IN BLOOM		
TASKS		
NOTES		

Bellflower cultivar (*Campanula* sp.)

JULY

JULY

YEAR		
WEATHER		
PLANTS IN BLOOM		
TASKS		
NOTES		

Verbascum blattaria

JULY

AUGUST

	YEAR		
WEATHER			
PLANTS IN BLOOM			
TASKS			
NOTES			

Cornflower cultivars (*Centaurea montana*)

AUGUST

AUGUST

YEAR		
WEATHER		
PLANTS IN BLOOM		
TASKS		
NOTES		

Two forms of *Ajuga pyramidalis*

AUGUST

AUGUST

	YEAR		
WEATHER			
PLANTS IN BLOOM			
TASKS			
NOTES			

Ranunculus cultivars

AUGUST

AUGUST

	YEAR		
WEATHER			
PLANTS IN BLOOM			
TASKS			
NOTES			

Larkspur cultivar (*Consolida regalis*)

AUGUST

AUGUST

YEAR		
WEATHER		
PLANTS IN BLOOM		
TASKS		
NOTES		

Calendula officinalis

AUGUST

SEPTEMBER

	YEAR		
WEATHER			
PLANTS IN BLOOM			
TASKS			
NOTES			

Varieties of sage (*Salvia horminum*)

SEPTEMBER

SEPTEMBER

	YEAR		
	WEATHER		
	PLANTS IN BLOOM		
	TASKS		
	NOTES		

Cultivars of snapdragon (*Antirrhinum majus*)

SEPTEMBER

SEPTEMBER

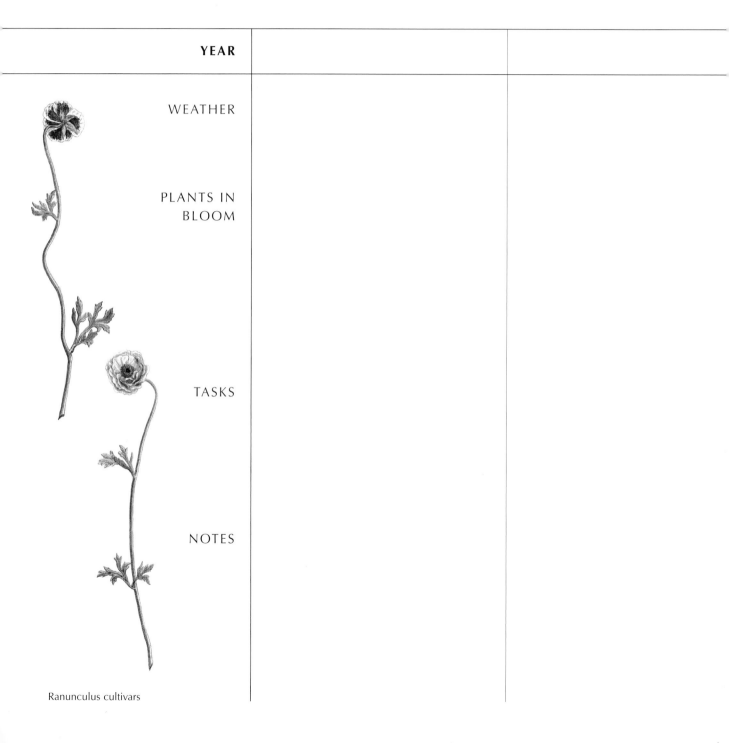

YEAR

WEATHER

PLANTS IN
BLOOM

TASKS

NOTES

Ranunculus cultivars

SEPTEMBER

SEPTEMBER

YEAR		
WEATHER		
PLANTS IN BLOOM		
TASKS		
NOTES		

Anemone cultivars

SEPTEMBER

SEPTEMBER

	YEAR	
WEATHER		
PLANTS IN BLOOM		
TASKS		
NOTES		

Gomphrena globosa

SEPTEMBER

OCTOBER

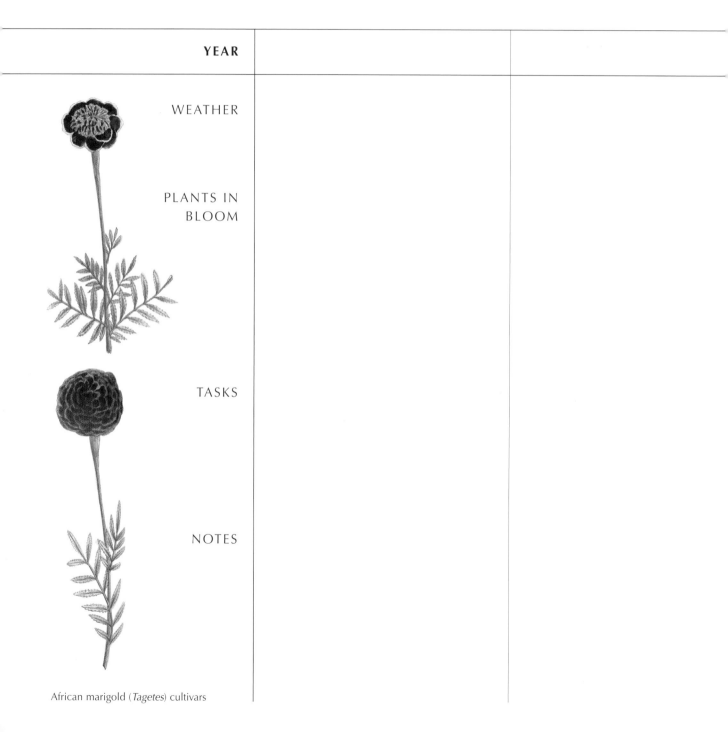

	YEAR		
	WEATHER		
	PLANTS IN BLOOM		
	TASKS		
	NOTES		

African marigold (*Tagetes*) cultivars

OCTOBER

OCTOBER

	YEAR		
WEATHER			
PLANTS IN BLOOM			
TASKS			
NOTES			

Marsh marigolds (*Caltha palustris*)

OCTOBER

OCTOBER

	YEAR		
	WEATHER		
	PLANTS IN BLOOM		
	TASKS		
	NOTES		

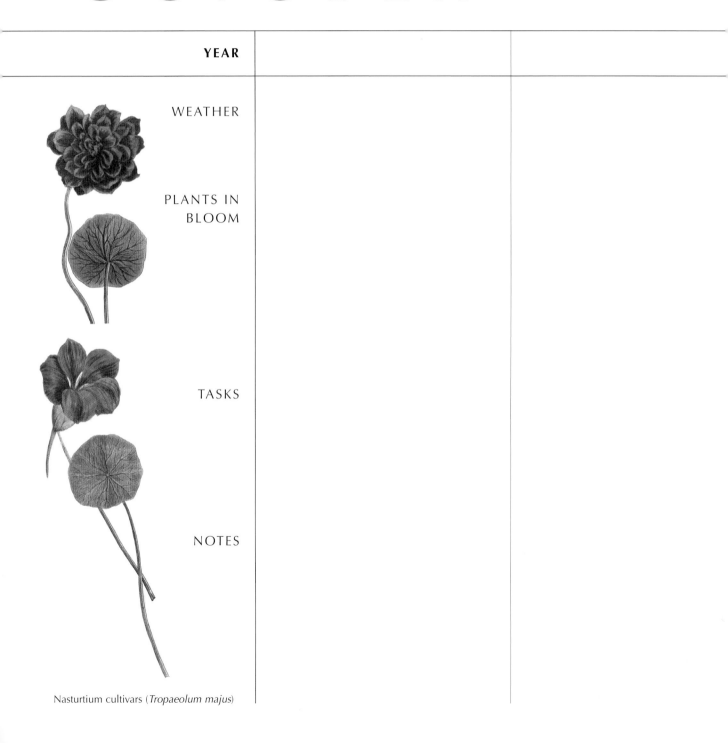

Nasturtium cultivars (*Tropaeolum majus*)

OCTOBER

OCTOBER

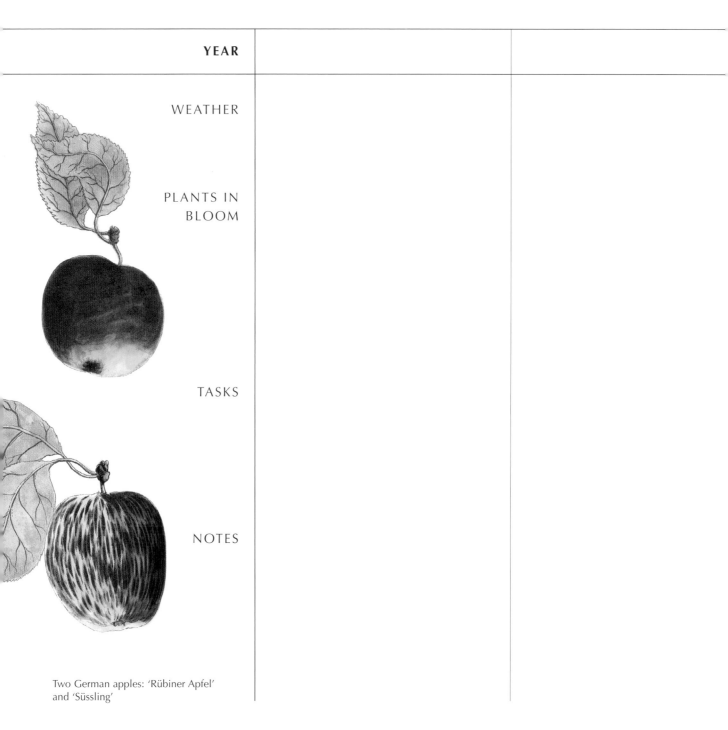

YEAR		
WEATHER		
PLANTS IN BLOOM		
TASKS		
NOTES		

Two German apples: 'Rübiner Apfel' and 'Süssling'

OCTOBER

OCTOBER

YEAR		
WEATHER		
PLANTS IN BLOOM		
TASKS		
NOTES		

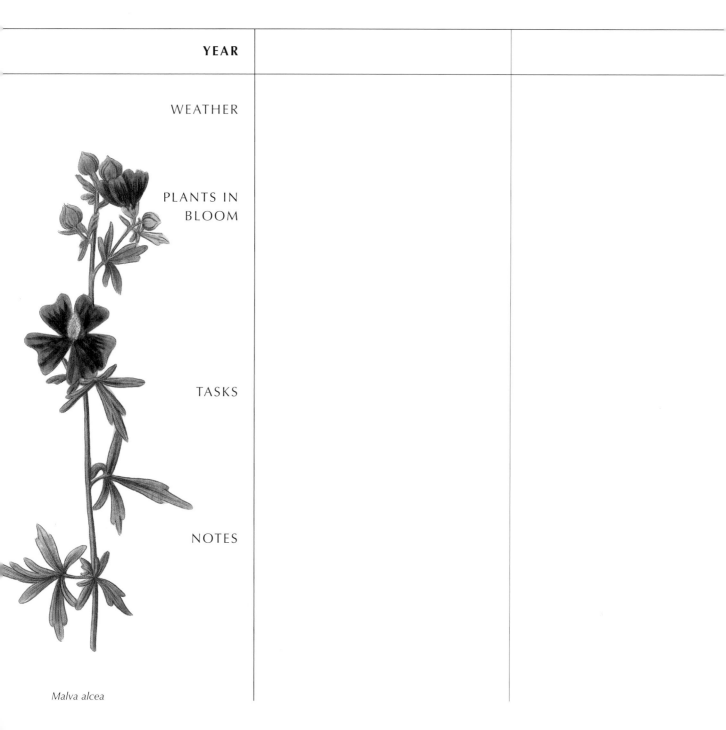

Malva alcea

OCTOBER

NOVEMBER

	YEAR	2014
	WEATHER	warm & showery 10°C - 14°C (14th)
	PLANTS IN BLOOM	Verbena Stipa Gigantica
	TASKS	14th most leaves down
	NOTES	

The orchid species *Limodorum abortivum*

NOVEMBER

NOVEMBER

	YEAR		
WEATHER			
PLANTS IN BLOOM			
TASKS			
NOTES			

Two pears: 'Coignacier' and 'Poire de Livre'

NOVEMBER

NOVEMBER

YEAR		
WEATHER		
PLANTS IN BLOOM		
TASKS		
NOTES		

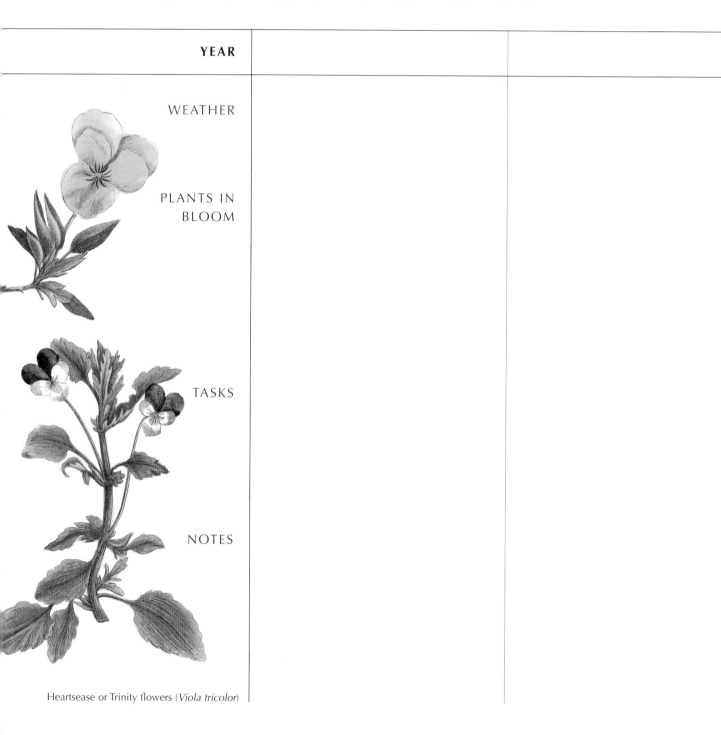

Heartsease or Trinity flowers (*Viola tricolor*)

NOVEMBER

NOVEMBER

YEAR		
WEATHER		
PLANTS IN BLOOM		
TASKS		
NOTES		

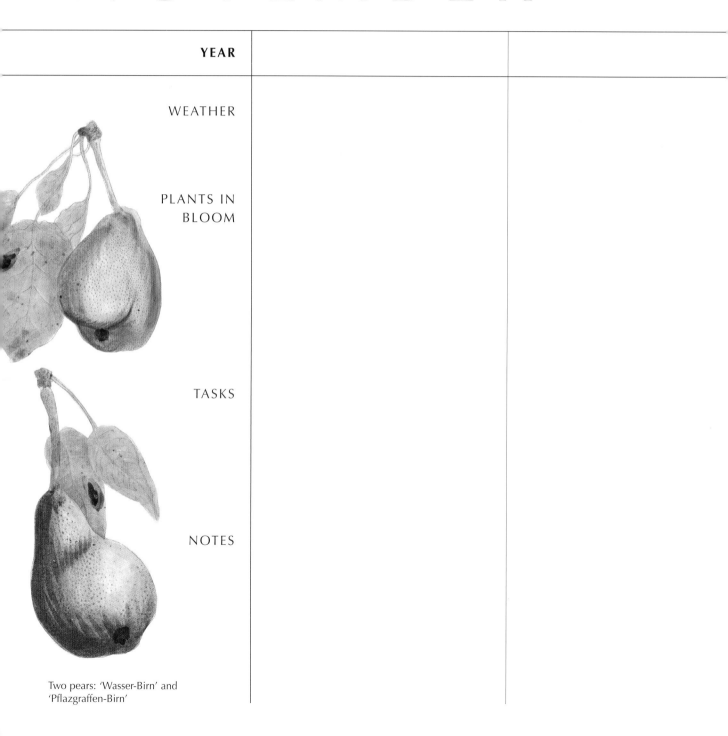

Two pears: 'Wasser-Birn' and
'Pflazgraffen-Birn'

NOVEMBER

NOVEMBER

YEAR		
WEATHER		
PLANTS IN BLOOM		
TASKS		
NOTES		

Calluna vulgaris

NOVEMBER

DECEMBER

	YEAR		
WEATHER			
PLANTS IN BLOOM			
TASKS			
NOTES			

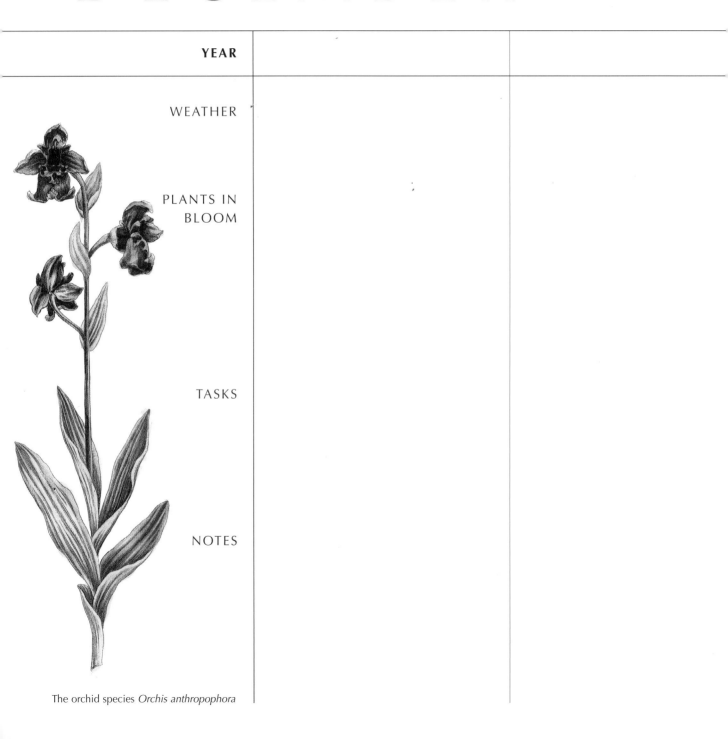

The orchid species *Orchis anthropophora*

DECEMBER

DECEMBER

YEAR		
WEATHER		
PLANTS IN BLOOM		
TASKS		
NOTES		

Heartsease or Trinity flowers (*Viola tricolor*)

DECEMBER

DECEMBER

	YEAR		
WEATHER			
PLANTS IN BLOOM			
TASKS			
NOTES			

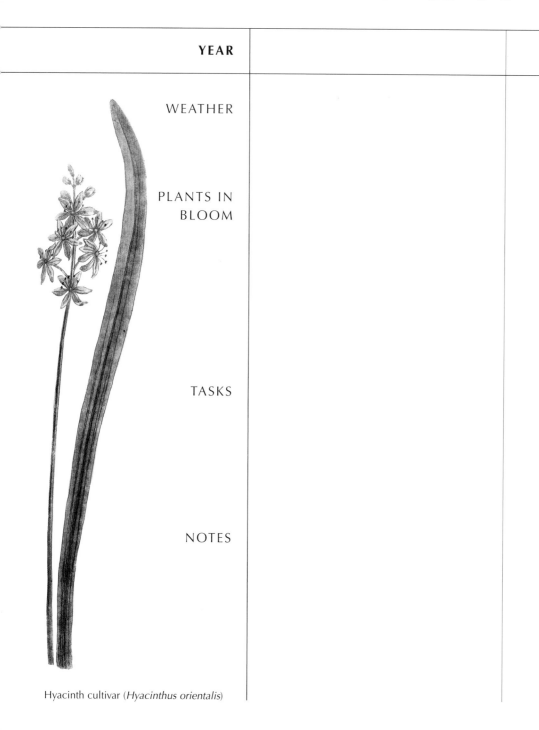

Hyacinth cultivar (*Hyacinthus orientalis*)

DECEMBER

DECEMBER

YEAR		
WEATHER		
PLANTS IN BLOOM		
TASKS		
NOTES		

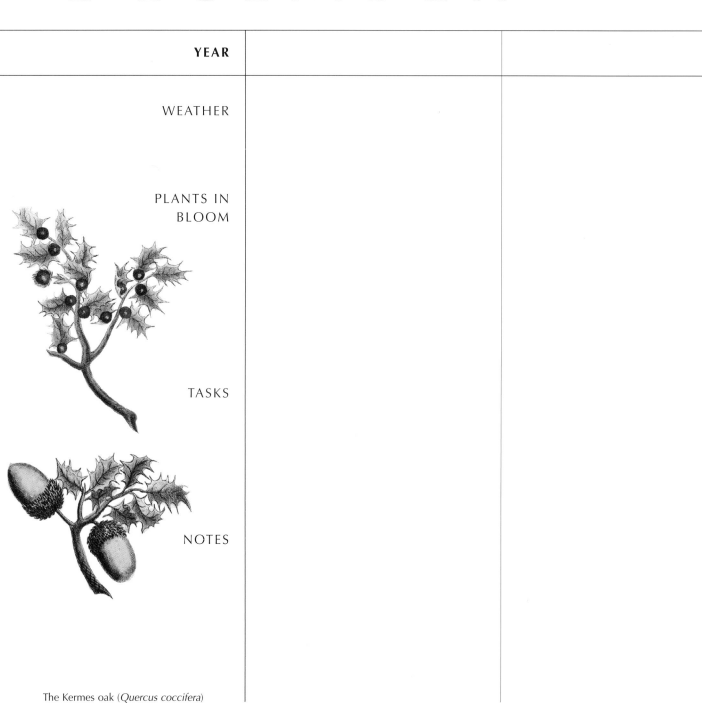

The Kermes oak (*Quercus coccifera*)

DECEMBER

DECEMBER

YEAR		
WEATHER		
PLANTS IN BLOOM		
TASKS		
NOTES		

Picea abies (above) and
Pinus sylvestris (below)

DECEMBER

PLANTS TO BUY

PLANT NAME	WHERE SEEN	SUPPLIER	PLANTING POSITION

PLANTS TO BUY

PLANT NAME	WHERE SEEN	SUPPLIER	PLANTING POSITION

PLANTS TO BUY

PLANT NAME	WHERE SEEN	SUPPLIER	PLANTING POSITION

PLANTS TO BUY

PLANT NAME	WHERE SEEN	SUPPLIER	PLANTING POSITION

PLANT SUPPLIERS

NAME	ADDRESS	TEL/FAX/E-MAIL

PLANT SUPPLIERS

NAME	ADDRESS	TEL/FAX/E-MAIL

PLANT SUPPLIERS

NAME	ADDRESS	TEL/FAX/E-MAIL

USEFUL ADDRESSES

NAME	ADDRESS	TEL/FAX/E-MAIL

GARDENS TO VISIT

GARDEN	WHEN TO VISIT	LOOK FOR

GARDENS TO VISIT

DATE VISITED	COMMENTS

GARDENS TO VISIT

GARDEN	WHEN TO VISIT	LOOK FOR

GARDENS TO VISIT

DATE VISITED	COMMENTS

NOTES